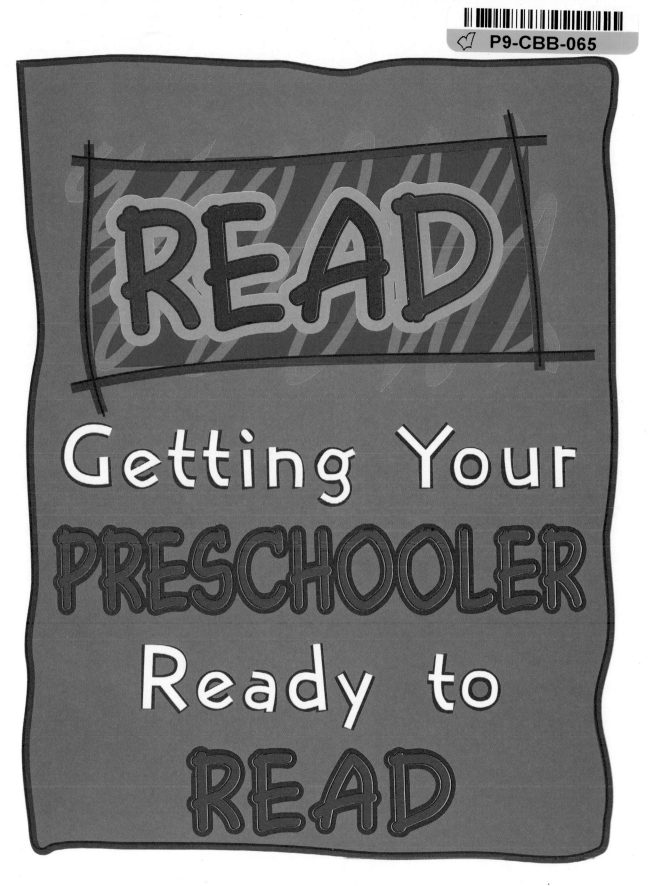

# READ

# Getting Your PRESCHOOLER Ready to READ

Michele Warrence-Schreiber

**Michele Warrence-Schreiber** holds a master's degree in reading education. She is a freelance writer of educational material and teaches kindergarten and elementary school reading. She has contributed to a variety of publications and video projects, including those for Scholastic, Houghton Mifflin, UNICEF, and PBS teacher development videos.

Illustrations by: George Ulrich

ISBN-13: 978-1-4127-1232-3

ISBN-10: 1-4127-1232-7

Manufactured in China.

8 7 6 5 4 3 2 1

# Contents

# Ready to Read

Dear Parents:

Preschool is an exciting time
for children. They seem to
want to know more about
everything! They are ready for
new challenges, such as
learning to read and write
letters, recognize words, and
put them together in simple
sentences. Of course you want to give your child a special
head start, which is so important. By using this workbook,
you will help your child learn the basic skills of a vast array
of reading concepts and processes—skills your child will
build on in school.

Inside this workbook, children will find fun-filled reading
activities. Each activity focuses on a different skill and
provides your child with opportunities to practice that skill.
The activities are arranged in order of difficulty, beginning
with the most basic skills at the front of the
workbook. This will help build your child's
confidence as he or she goes along. Your child will
feel a real sense of accomplishment after
completing each page.

Every activity is clearly labeled with the skill
being taught. Skill keys written for you, the
parent, are at the bottom of the page. These

skill keys give you information about what your child is learning and a foundation for discussion with teachers.

Children learn in a variety of ways. The bright, engaging illustrations in this workbook will help visual learners develop their reading skills by showing letters and words in context.

Children may also like to touch and trace the letters and words and say them out loud. Each of these methods can be an important aid in your child's learning process. Have markers and a pencil and paper at the ready— the more practice your child gets, the better. He or she will enjoy putting these new skills to work.

Help your child with the simple directions for each activity, then encourage the child to try the exercise on their own. Each activity should be fun and enough of a challenge that it will be enticing for your child. Be patient and support your child in positive ways. Let them know it's all right to take a guess or pull back if they're unsure. And, of course, celebrate their successes with them.

Read every day! Reading together is fun for both of you. Learning should be an exciting and positive experience for everyone. Enjoy your time together as your child learns to love reading!

# Which Way Is Up?

One of these children is ready to read! Circle the picture that shows the child holding the book **right side up.**

Skill: Understanding basic concept **right side up**

# Left to Right

Trace the lines from left to right to help the animals get home.

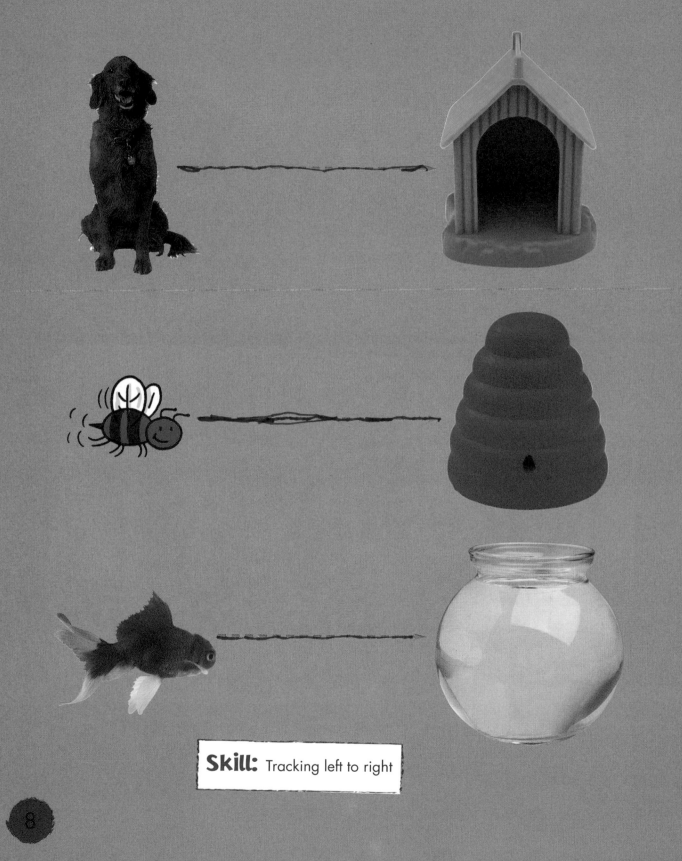

# Find the Food

Trace the lines from left to right to help the animals get their food.

**Skill:** Tracking left to right

# Top to Bottom

Help the children come down. Trace the lines from top to bottom to help the children in the playground.

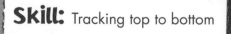

**Skill:** Tracking top to bottom

# Coming Down!

These firefighters need to get to the bottom of their poles in a hurry! Help them by tracing the lines from top to bottom.

**Skill:** Tracking top to bottom

11

# Under Here, Under There

Look at the picture. The mouse is **under** the table. Can you draw a cat under the table?

**Skill:** Understanding positional word **under**

# Over the Top!

Circle the picture that shows the airplane is **over** the cloud.

Circle the picture that shows the bee is **over** the flower.

**Skill:** Understanding positional word **over**

13

# In and Out

Dad needs to go to the store. Draw a line to help him get **in** the car.

Now draw a line to help the dog come **out** of the doghouse to play with the ball.

**Skill:** Understanding positional words **in** and **out**

# Monkey in the Middle

Put a circle around the monkey in the **middle.**

Put an X through the dog in the **middle.**

**Skill:** Understanding positional word **middle**

# Stranded!

Help the girl get to the other side of the river. Draw a bridge for her to go **across** the river.

Is there another way to get **across** the river? Put a circle around the boat to show the girl how to get to the other side.

**Skill:** Understanding positional word **across**

# Treasure Hunt

Go **through** the maze to find the treasure. First use your finger. Then use a pencil.

# Same

Color the two pictures in each row that are the **same.**

**Skill:** Matching identical objects

# Same Old, Same Old

Circle the picture that is the **same** as the first picture in each row.

**Skill:** Matching identical objects

# Different

Circle the picture that is **different** in each row.

**Skill:** Identifying different objects

# The Difference Is Clear

Put an **X** through the picture that is **different** in each row.

21

# Hot or Cold?

Look at the pictures. Color all the **hot** things **red.** Color all the **cold** things **blue.**

**Skill:** Understanding opposites

# Opposites Attract

Look at the pictures. Draw a line between each pair of **opposites.**

small

empty

wet

big

full

dry

# Go-Togethers

Look at the pictures. Circle the picture that goes with the first picture in each row.

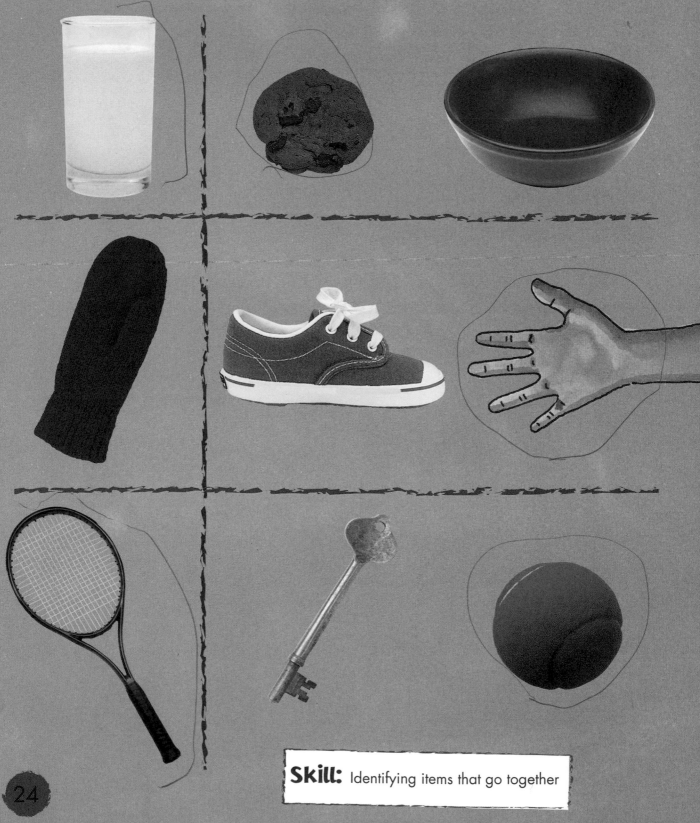

24

# Write Your Name

You can write your name! Ask someone to write your name on the the first name tag. Then you can trace over it. Now try to write your name all by yourself!

HELLO
my name is

LONYIN

HELLO
my name is

KENINLee

**Skill:** Recognizing and writing a name

# The ABCs

There are 26 letters in the alphabet. Look at each letter and trace it with your finger.

# A, B, C

Trace the letters **A, B,** and **C.** Then write the letters yourself.

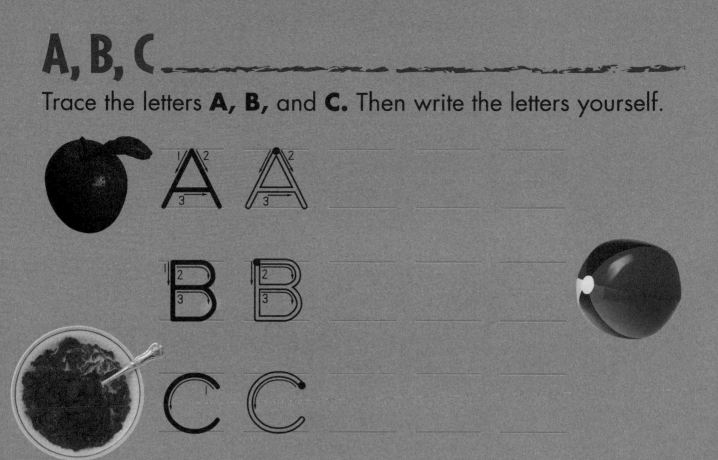

The word **ANIMAL** begins with the letter **A.** Draw a picture of your favorite animal.

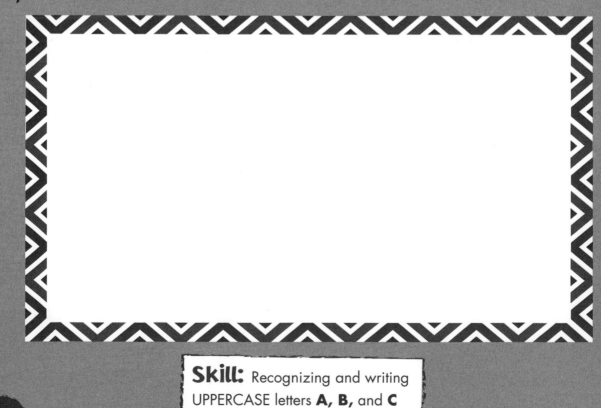

**Skill:** Recognizing and writing UPPERCASE letters **A, B,** and **C**

# D, E, F

Help the frog cross the pond! Color the lily pads with the letters **D, E,** and **F** to show the way. Then trace and write the letters below.

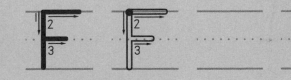

**Skill:** Recognizing and writing UPPERCASE letters **D, E,** and **F**

29

# G, H, I

Look at the first letter in each row. Circle the letter that is the same as the first one.

| G | G | A |
|---|---|---|
| H | E | H |
| I | I | C |

Now trace and write the letters.

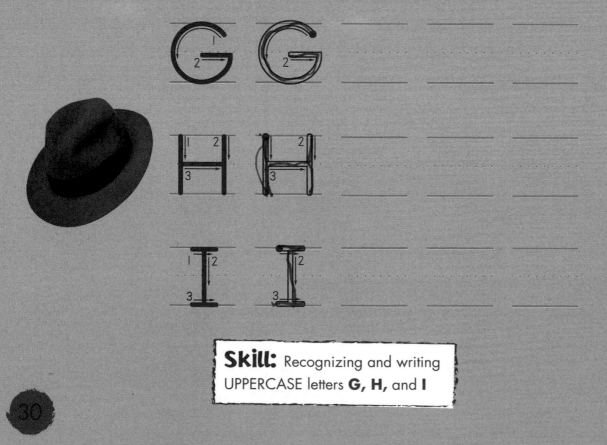

G G

H H

I I

**Skill:** Recognizing and writing UPPERCASE letters **G, H,** and **I**

# J, K, L

Color the shapes to find a hidden picture! Color each space with a **J red.** Color each space with a **K blue.** Color each space with an **L green.**

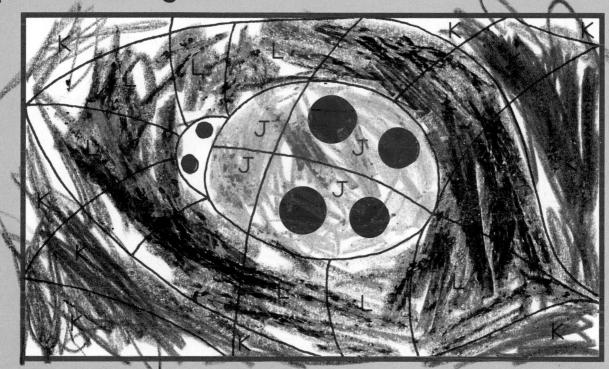

Now trace and write the letters.

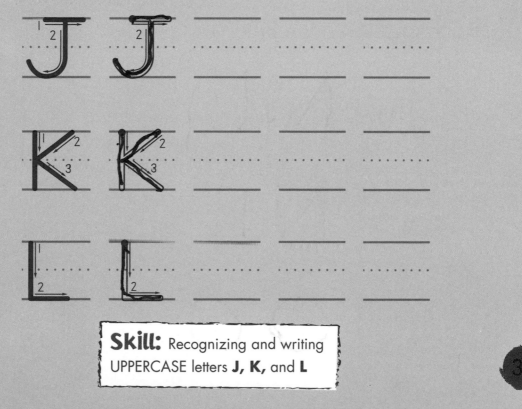

31

# M, N, O

Can you find the letters in this bowl of alphabet soup? Color each **M yellow.** Color each **N blue.** Color each **O green.**

Now trace and write the letters.

M  M  N
N  N  N
O  O  O

# Letter Review

Connect the dots in order of the alphabet from **A** to **O.** Then color the picture.

# P, Q, R

Draw a line from each letter on the left to the matching letter on the right.

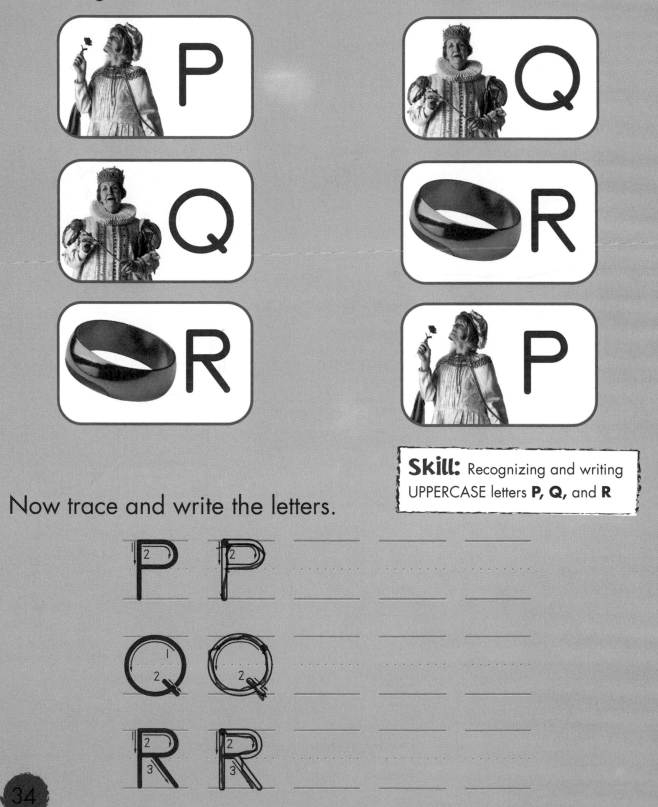

Now trace and write the letters.

34

# S, T, U

Help the boy dry his hands! Color the trail of soap bubbles with the letters **S, T,** and **U** to get to the towel.

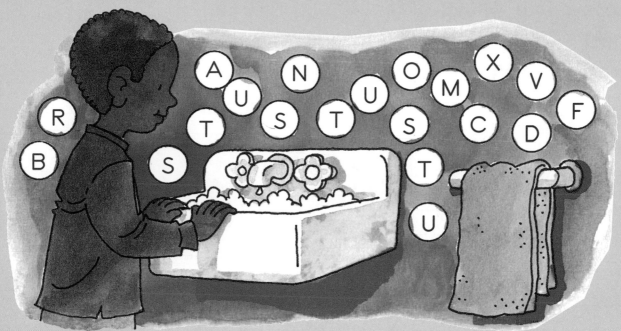

Now trace and write the letters.

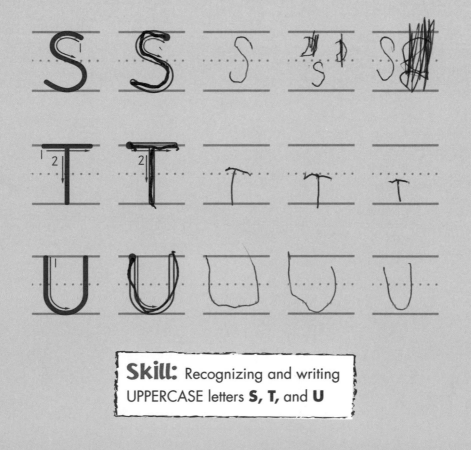

**Skill:** Recognizing and writing UPPERCASE letters **S, T,** and **U**

# V, W, X

The flowers in this vase aren't quite finished! Create a beautiful bouquet by coloring the flower marked with a **V pink,** the flower marked with a **W purple,** and the flower marked with an **X yellow.** Then draw your own flower in the middle.

**Skill:** Recognizing and writing UPPERCASE letters **V, W,** and **X**

Now trace and write the letters.

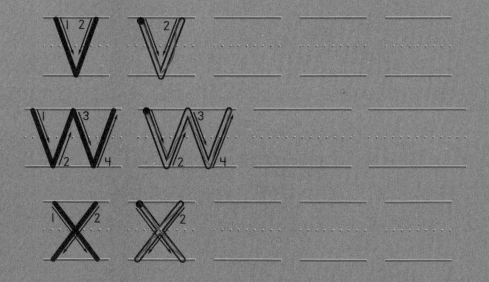

# Y and Z

Trace the letters **Y** and **Z.** Then write the letters yourself.

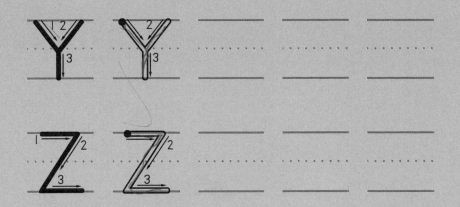

The word **ZEBRA** begins with the letter **Z.** Draw a picture of a zebra.

I LOVE YOU

# A to Z

Help the squirrel find the tree! Follow the path in order from **A** to **Z** to show the way.

# What Comes Next?

Fill in the blanks and help the children write the whole alphabet in order!

# a, b, c

Each letter in the alphabet can be written in UPPERCASE or lowercase. Look at the lowercase letters in each row. Find the letter that is the same as the first letter in each row and put a circle around it.

|     |     |     |
|-----|-----|-----|
| a   | z   | a   |
| b   | b   | f   |
| c   | c   | q   |

Now trace and write the letters.

a²   a²

b   b

c   c

**Skill:** Recognizing and writing lowercase letters **a, b,** and **c**

42

# Balloon, Balloon!

Help the children get their balloons! The UPPERCASE letter on each balloon has a matching lowercase letter on a child's shirt. Draw a line to give each child a balloon with the letter that matches.

**Skill:** Matching UPPERCASE and lowercase letters

# d, e, f

Draw a line from the letter on the left to connect it with the matching letter on the right.

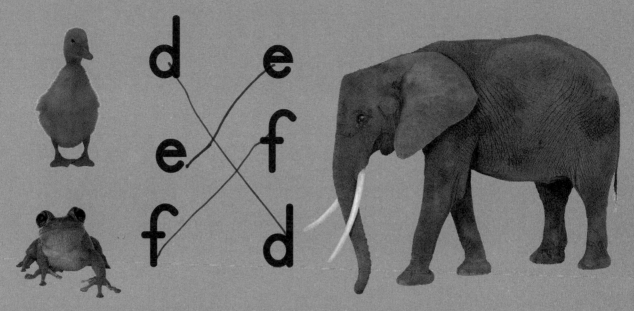

d

e

f

d    e

f

d

Now trace and write the letters.

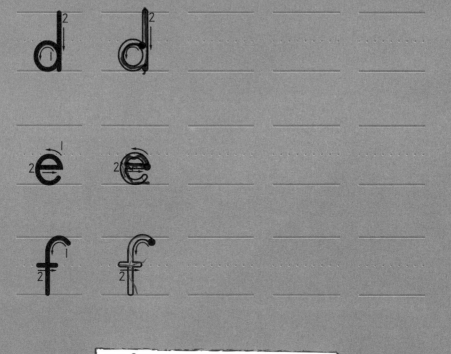

# Family Reunion

Help each baby animal find their parent. Draw a line from each lowercase letter to the matching UPPERCASE letter.

**Skill:** Matching UPPERCASE and lowercase letters

# g, h, i

What's hidden in this picture? Find all the spaces marked with a **g** and color them **green.** Find all the spaces marked with an **h** and color them **red.** Find all the spaces marked with an **i** and color them **blue.**

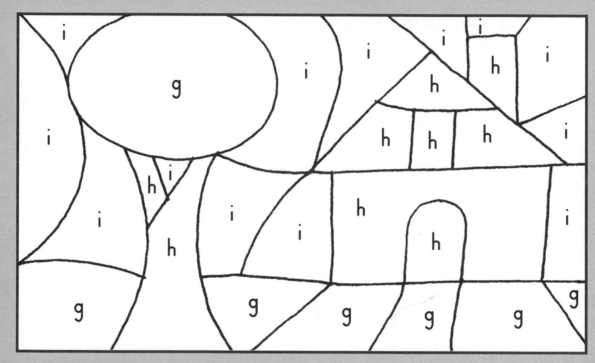

Now trace and write the letters.

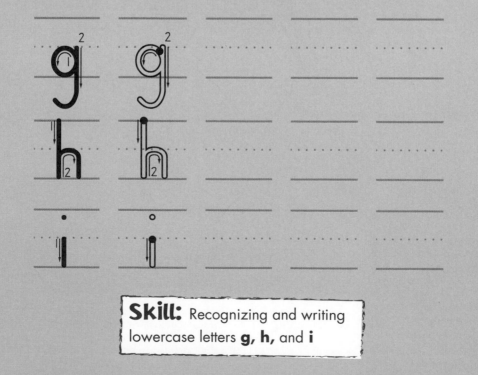

Skill: Recognizing and writing lowercase letters **g, h,** and **i**

# Ice Cream!

Color the ice-cream cones that have matching UPPERCASE and lowercase letters.

# j, k, l

Find the key to open the locks! Each key has a letter on it that is the same as the letter on one of the locks. Draw a line from each key to the lock with the matching letter.

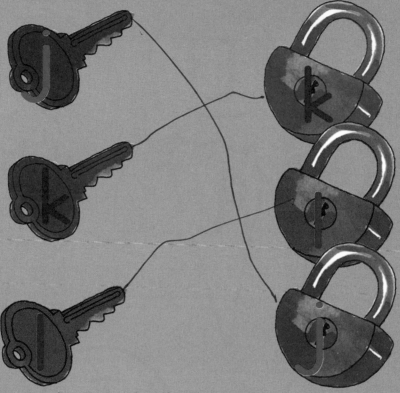

Now trace and write the letters.

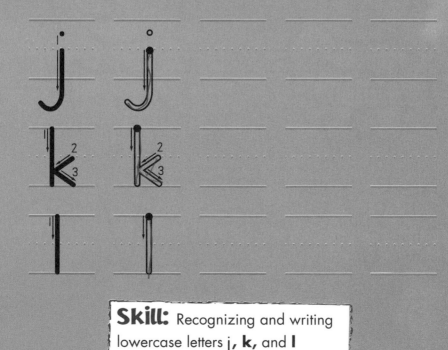

48

# Send a Letter

Match the lowercase letter on each stamp to its UPPERCASE letter on an envelope. Color each matching envelope and stamp a different color.

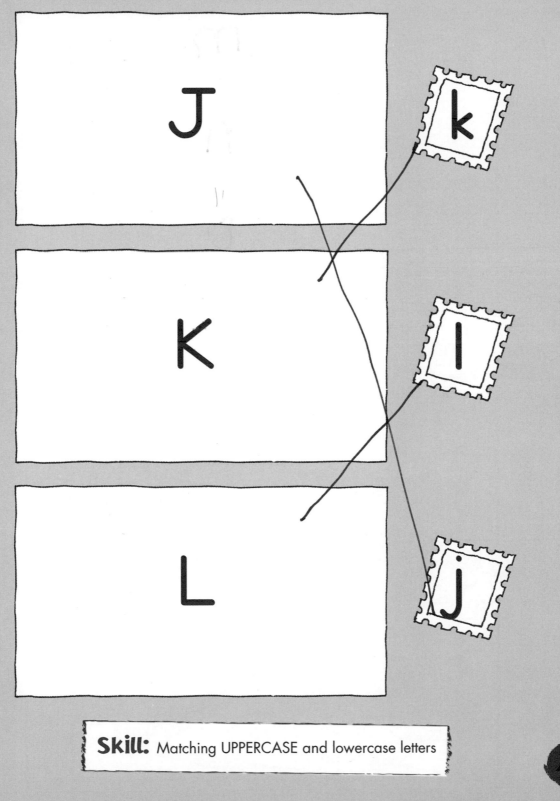

# m, n, o

Help the girl get to her radio. Color the music notes marked **m, n,** and **o** to find the way. Then trace and write the letters.

**Skill:** Recognizing and writing lowercase letters **m, n,** and **o**

50

# Make a Match!

Draw a line from each card with an UPPERCASE letter to the card with the matching lowercase letter.

# p, q, r.

It's raining! Help the queen stay dry by finishing the umbrella. Color the space marked with a **p purple.** Color the space marked with a **q yellow.** Color the space marked with an **r red.**

Now trace and write the letters.

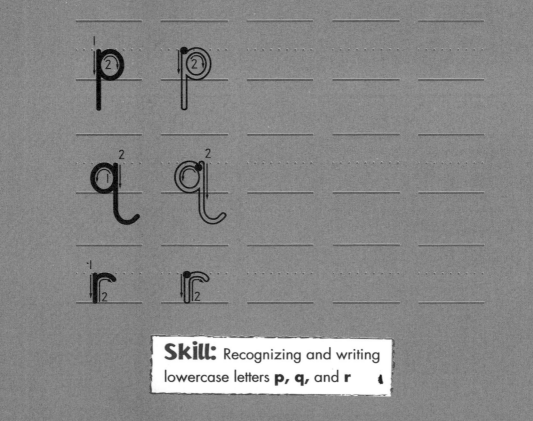

# Time to Paint

Find the right brush to use with each color of paint! Draw a line from each paint can with an UPPERCASE letter to the brush with the matching lowercase letter. Now color each brush the same color as the matching paint can.

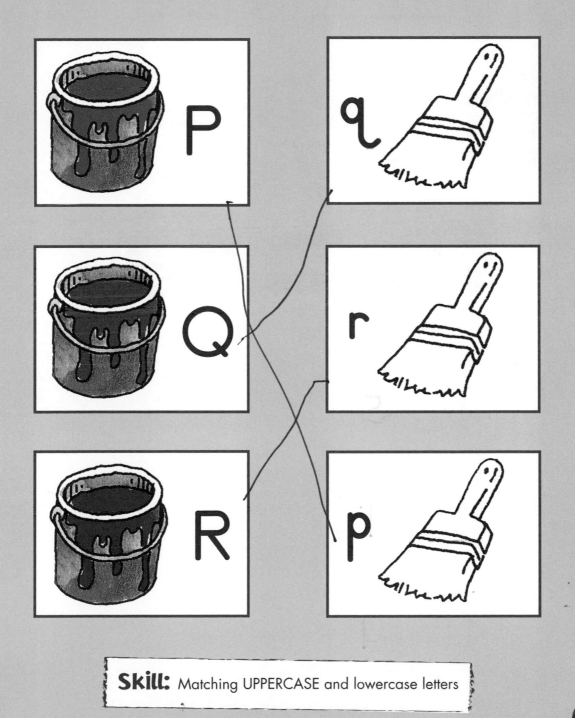

**Skill:** Matching UPPERCASE and lowercase letters

# s, t, u

Look at the letters in each row. Circle the letter that is the same as the first letter in each row.

s    f    s

t    t    d

u    u    m

Now trace and write the letters.

s    s

t    t

u    u

Skill: Recognizing and writing lowercase letters **s, t,** and **u**

54

# Tic-Tac-Toe

Make an X through each square that has a matching UPPERCASE and lowercase letter. Can you get a tic-tac-toe?

|  |  |  |
|---|---|---|
| Uu | By | Qi |
| Am | Tt | Pr |
| Dc | Hg | Ss |

# V, W, X

Help the spider cross the web! Color the **v**, **w**, and **x** to show the way.

Now trace and write the letters.

**Skill:** Recognizing and writing lowercase letters **v**, **w**, and **x**

# Sweet Valentine

Color the valentine cards that have matching UPPERCASE and lowercase letters.

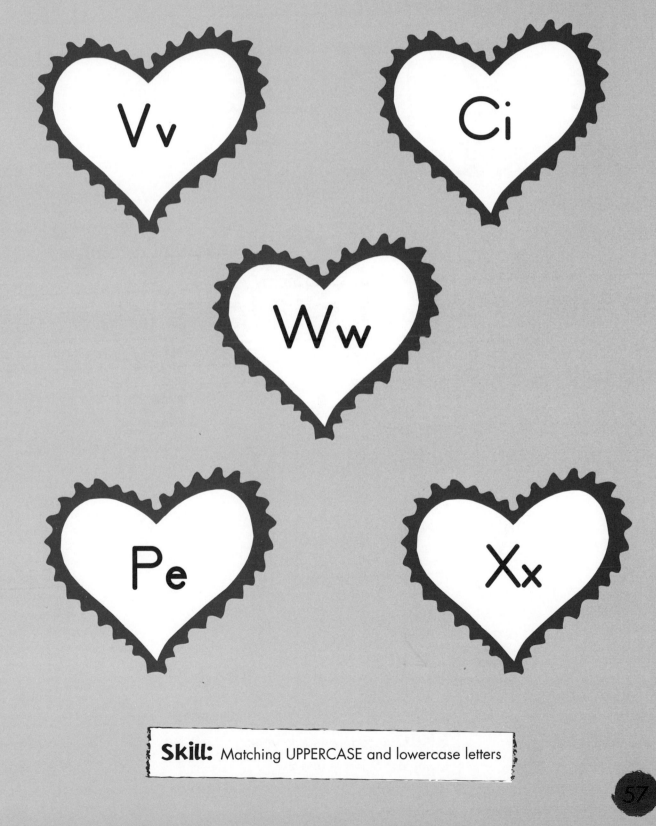

# y and z

Look at the letters in each row. Find the letter that is the same as the first letter in each row and put a circle around it.

y    a    y

z    z    t

Now trace and write the letters.

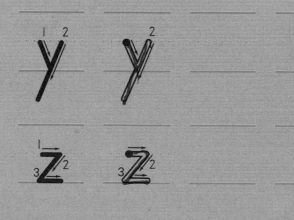

# Yo-yo

The UPPERCASE letter on each yo-yo has a matching lowercase letter on a child's shirt. Draw a string to give each child a yo-yo with the letter that matches.

Skill: Matching UPPERCASE and lowercase letters

# Connect the abcs!

What kind of animal is in this picture? Connect the dots from **a** to **z** to find out!

**Skill:** Using alphabetical order

60

# Letters Make Words!

Look at the words **cat** and **dog**. Each word is made of three letters. Put a circle around each letter in the word and say it out loud.

cat     dog

**Skill:** Understanding that letters form words

# Letter or Word?

Color the presents that have **words** on them.

car

b

ball

e

k

fish

**Skill:** Distinguishing between letters and words

# Spaces Are the Places

Spaces go between words to make them easy to read. Draw a line in the spaces between the words below. The first one is done for you.

**Skill:** Understanding that spaces separate words

# Red

Use a **red** crayon to color all the pictures with the word **red** on them.

Now trace and write the word **red.**

red

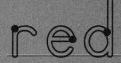

# Blue

Find the hidden picture! Use a **blue** crayon to color all the spaces with the word **blue** on them. Color the other spaces whatever color you like.

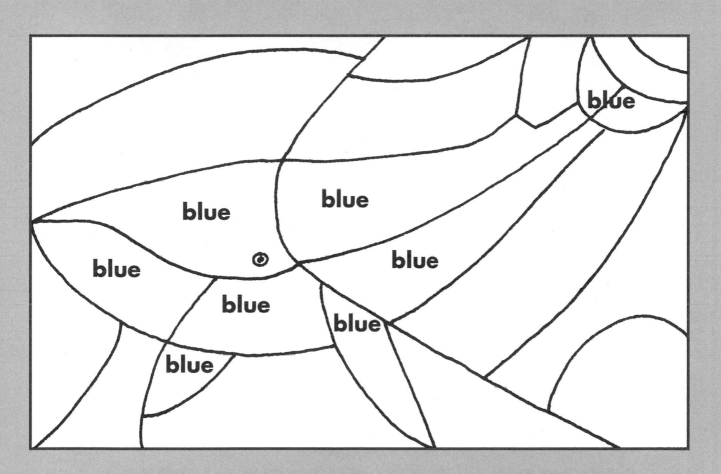

Now trace and write the word **blue.**

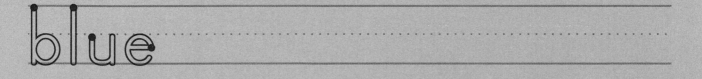

# Green

Each of the pictures below is of something **green.** Can you draw something **green?**

Now trace and write the word **green.**

green

# Yellow

Circle the **yellow** picture in each row.

Now trace and write the word **yellow.**

yellow

# Orange

Find all the oranges in the tree! Color each one with an **orange** crayon.

Now trace and write the word **orange.**

orange

**Skill:** Identifying colors and color words

# Purple

Circle the **purple** picture in each row.

Now trace and write the word **purple.**

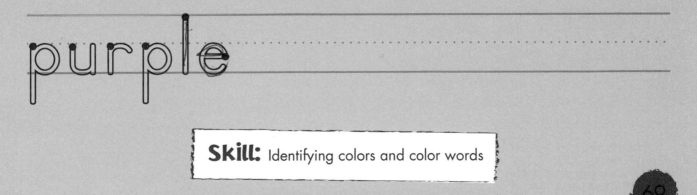

# Pink

Each of the pictures below is of something **pink.** Can you draw a pink pig in the box?

Now trace and write the word **pink.**

Skill: Identifying colors and color words

# Jelly Beans!

Draw a line to match each jelly bean on the left to the crayon with the same color on the right.

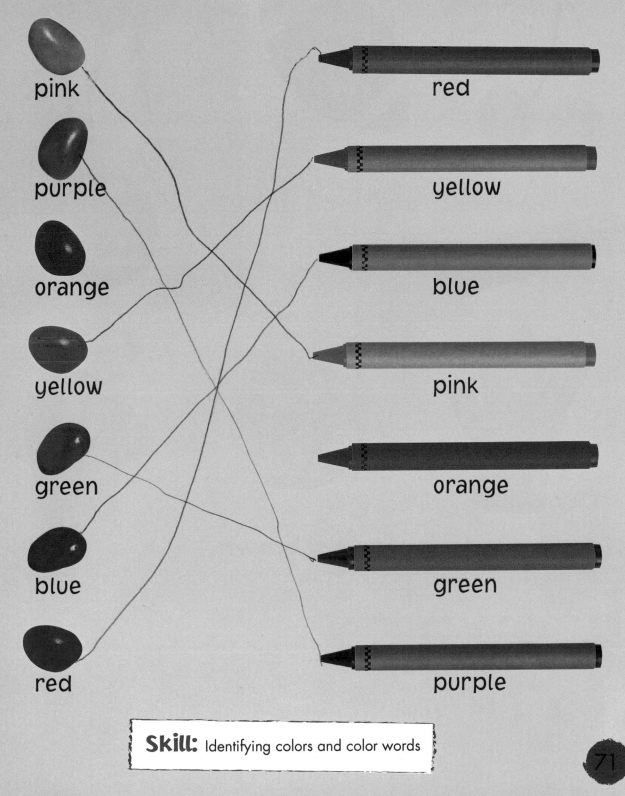

pink

purple

orange

yellow

green

blue

red

red

yellow

blue

pink

orange

green

purple

# Brown

Circle the **brown** picture in each row.

Now trace and write the word **brown.**

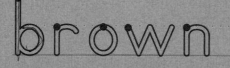

# Black

Find the hidden picture! Use a **black** crayon to color all the spaces with the word **black** on them. Color the other spaces whatever color you like.

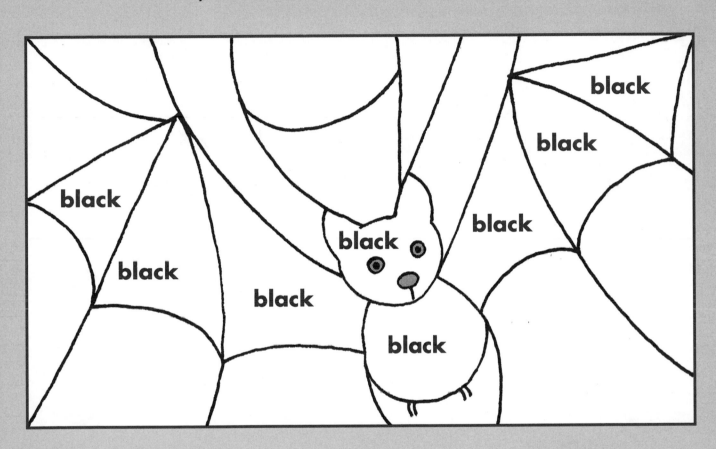

Now trace and write the word **black.**

black

73

# White

Each of the pictures below is of something **white.** Can you draw something white?

Now trace and write the word **white.**

white

# Gray

Help the elephant get through the maze to the circus tent!
Follow the **gray** pictures to show the way.

Now trace and write the word **gray.**

gray

**Skill:** Identifying colors and color words

# Color Review

Draw a line from each color word on the left to the crayon with the matching color on the right.

black

gray

brown

white

# B Is for Bat

Say the name of each picture. Circle the pictures that start with the **b** sound that you hear in the word **bat.**

# C Is for Cat and City

The letter **c** makes two sounds. Say the name of each picture. Color the pictures that start with the hard **c** sound that you hear in the word **cat.**

The word **city** starts with a soft **c** sound. Can you draw a picture of a city?

**Skills:** Identifying objects that begin with the **c** sound; identifying hard and soft sounds of **c**

# D Is for Dog

Say the name of each picture. Circle the picture in each row that starts with the **d** sound that you hear in the word **dog.**

**Skill:** Identifying objects that begin with the **d** sound

# F Is for Fish

These kids aren't just trying to catch fish! Say the name of the picture in each circle. Draw a line from the end of each child's fishing pole to a picture that starts with the **f** sound you hear in the word **fish.**

**Skill:** Identifying objects that begin with the **f** sound

# G Is for Goose and Giraffe

The letter **g** makes two sounds. Look at the pictures. Circle two animals that start with the hard **g** sound that you hear in the word **goose.**

Sometimes the letter **g** makes a different sound. The word **giraffe** starts with a soft **g** sound. Can you say **giraffe?** Draw a giraffe here.

**Skills:** Identifying objects that begin with the **g** sound; identifying hard and soft sounds of **g**

# What's that Sound?

Say the name of each picture. Circle the picture in each row that begins with the sound of the letter.

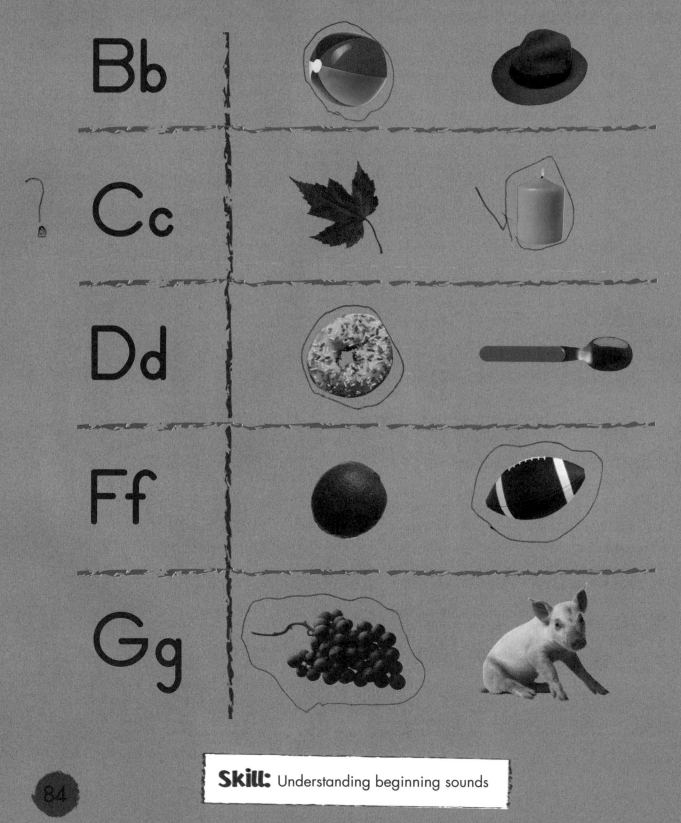

**Skill:** Understanding beginning sounds

# H Is for Hello

Say the name of each picture. Write the letter **h** under the two pictures in each row that start with the **h** sound that you hear in the word **hello.**

# J Is for Jump

The word **j**ump starts with the j sound. Can you say **j**ump? What else starts with a j sound? Use an **orange** crayon to color all the spaces marked j in the picture to find out!

**Skill:** Identifying objects that begin with the j sound

# K Is for Kite

The word **kite** starts with the **k** sound. Can you say **kite?** The word **kangaroo** also starts with the **k** sound. Can you say **kangaroo?** Can you draw a silly picture of a kangaroo flying a kite?

**Skill:** Identifying objects that begin with the **k** sound

# L Is for Lime

The word **lime** starts with the **l** sound. Can you say **lime?**
What else starts with the **l** sound? Connect the dots from **A** to
**Z** to find out.

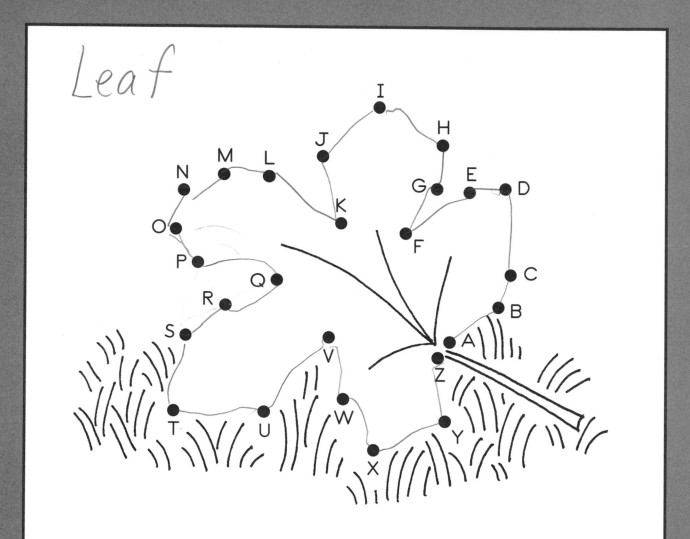

Leaf

# M Is for Monkey

**Monkey** starts with the **m** sound. Can you say **monkey?**
Draw a monkey in the box.

**Skill:** Identifying objects that begin with the **m** sound

# N Is for Night

Say the name of each picture. Color the stars with pictures that start with the **n** sound that you hear in the word **night.**

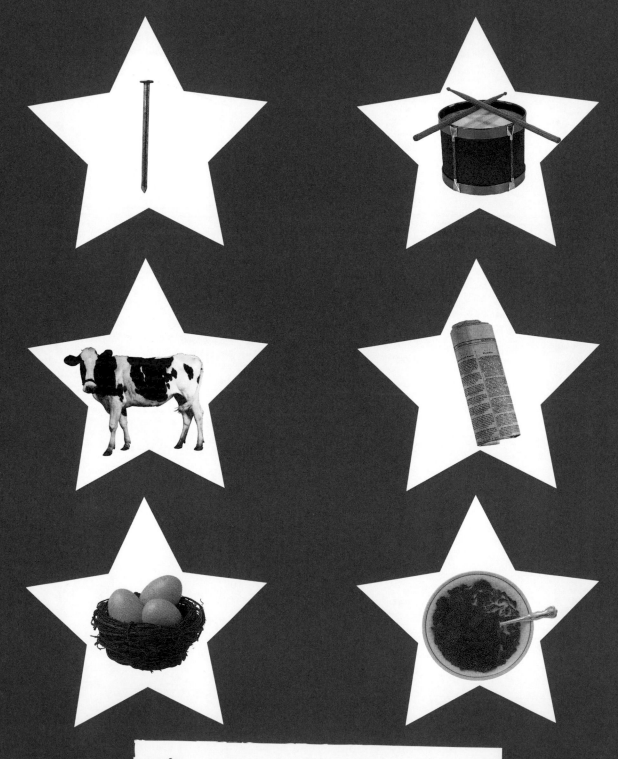

**Skill:** Identifying objects that begin with the **n** sound

# Sounds Tasty!

Say the name of each food or drink. Draw a line from each picture on the left to the letter you hear at the beginning of the word.

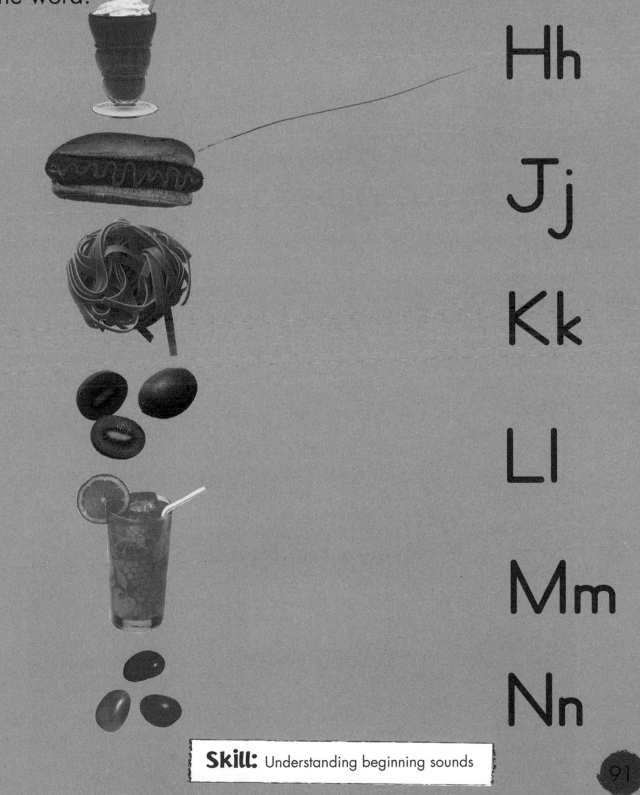

Hh

Jj

Kk

Ll

Mm

Nn

# P Is for Pig

Say the name of each picture. Write the letter **p** under the two pictures in each row that start with the **p** sound that you hear in the word **pig.**

**Skill:** Identifying objects that begin with the **p** sound

# Q Is for Queen

Look at the pictures in each square of the quilt. Use a **red** crayon to color the squares with pictures that start with the **q** sound that you hear in the word **queen.** Color the other squares **blue.**

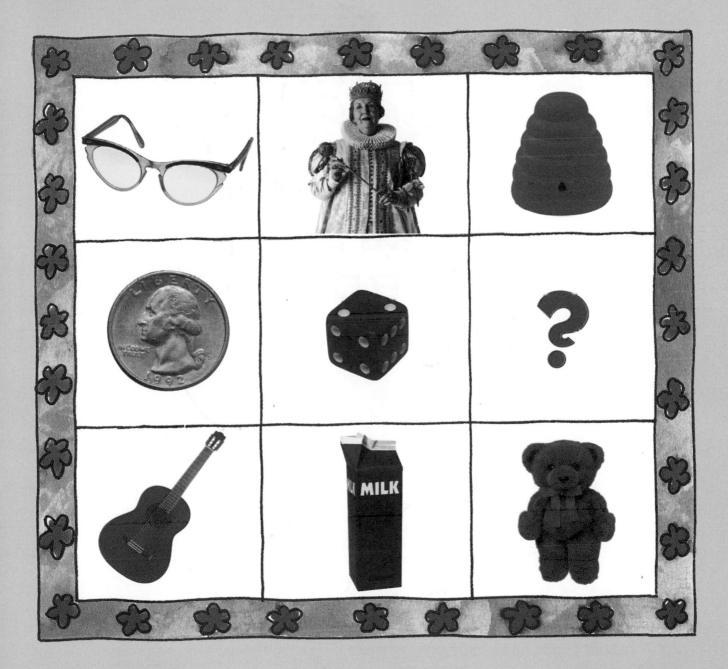

# R Is for Rain

The word **rain** starts with the **r** sound. Can you say **rain?**
What else starts with the **r** sound? Connect the dots from **A** to
**Z** to find out.

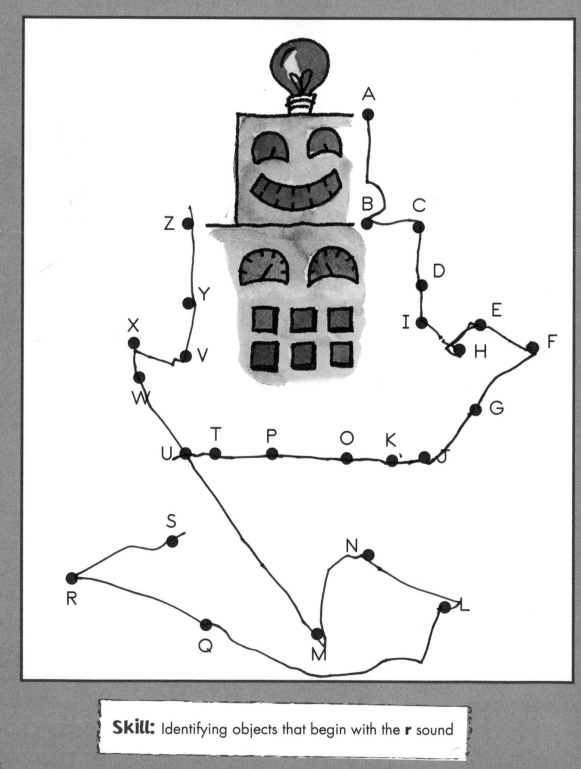

Skill: Identifying objects that begin with the **r** sound

# S Is for Sun

The word **sun** starts with the **s** sound. Can you say **sun?**
Draw a picture that shows you doing something fun on a
sunny day.

**Skill:** Identifying objects that begin with the **s** sound

# T Is for Top

The word **top** starts with the **t** sound. Can you say **top?**
Look at the picture. Circle at least three things that start
with the sound of **t.**

**Skill:** Identifying objects that begin with the **t** sound

96

# A Sound Match

Say the name of each picture. Circle the picture in each row that begins with the sound of the letter.

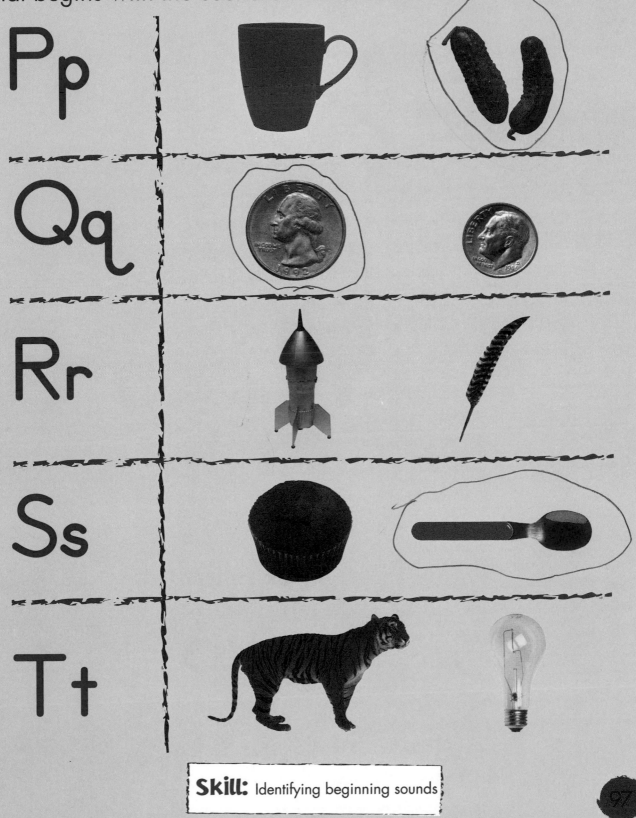

**Pp**

**Qq**

**Rr**

**Ss**

**Tt**

Skill: Identifying beginning sounds

# V Is for Vase

Say the name of each picture. Circle the picture in each row that starts with the **v** sound that you hear in the word **vase.**

**Skill:** Identifying objects that begin with the **v** sound

# W Is for Wallet

Say the name of each picture. Write the letter **w** under the two pictures in each row that start with the **w** sound that you hear in the word **wallet.**

# X Is for X-ray

The word **x-ray** starts with the **x** sound. Can you say **x-ray?**

Most words do not start with **x.** The **x** is usually found in the middle or at the end of the word.

Say the name of each picture. Do you hear the **x** sound? Draw a line under the **x** in each word.

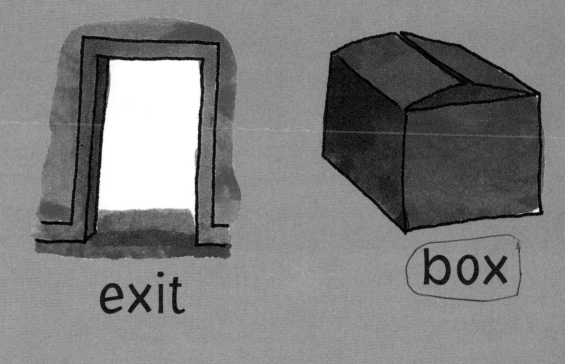

exit

box

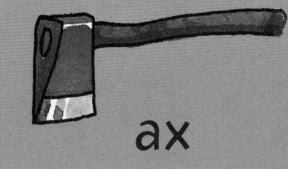

ax

**Skill:** Identifying objects that have the **x** sound

# Y Is for Yellow

Say the name of each picture. Circle the picture in each row that starts with the **y** sound that you hear in the word **yellow**.

STRAWBERRY YOGURT

Skill: Identifying objects that begin with the **y** sound

# Z Is for Zebra

Help the zebra get to the zoo! Say the name of each circled picture. Color the circles that have objects that start with the **z** sound you hear in the word **zebra** to help it find the way.

zero

**Skill:** Identifying objects that begin with the **z** sound

# What Wonderful Sounds!

Say the name of each picture. Draw a line from each picture on the left to the letter you hear at the beginning of the word.

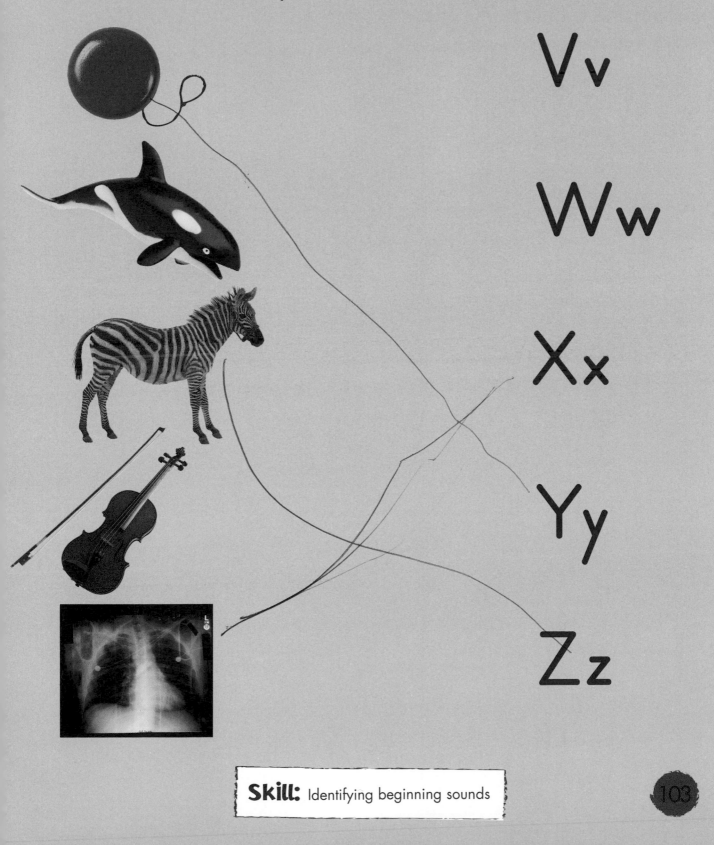

Vv

Ww

Xx

Yy

Zz

# Vowels

There are five special letters in the alphabet. They are called **vowels.** The sounds they make are called **vowel sounds.** Color the pictures in each row and say their names to hear some of the vowel sounds.

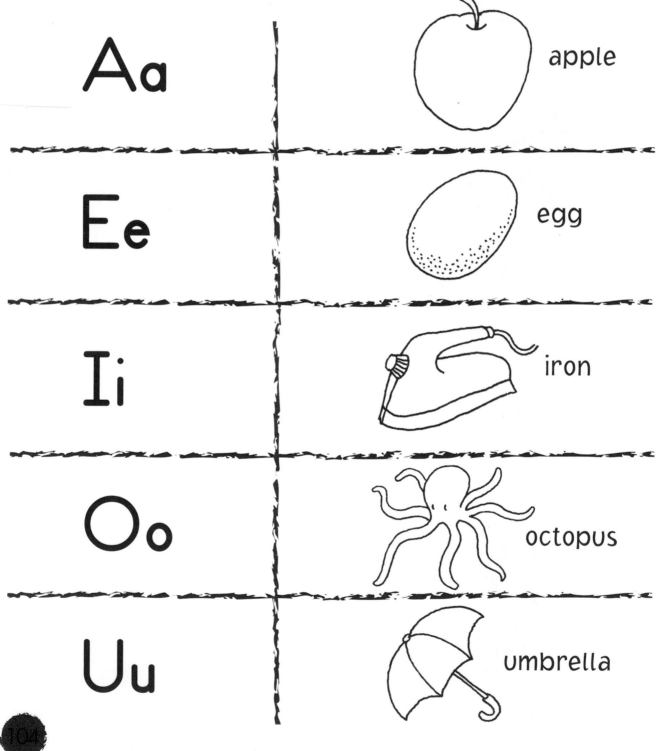

| | |
|---|---|
| Aa | apple |
| Ee | egg |
| Ii | iron |
| Oo | octopus |
| Uu | umbrella |

**Skill:** Understanding beginning sounds for vowels

ax

ape

elephant

ear

ice cream

igloo

orange

oval

umpire

uniform

# A Is for Animal and Acorn

Say the name of each picture. Write the letter **a** under the two pictures in each row that start with the short **a** sound that you hear in the word **animal.**

Sometimes the letter **a** makes a different sound. The word **acorn** starts with a long **a** sound. Can you say **acorn?** Draw an acorn here.

# E Is for Egg and Eat

The word **egg** starts with a short **e** sound. Can you say **egg?** What else starts with the short **e** sound? Connect the dots to find out.

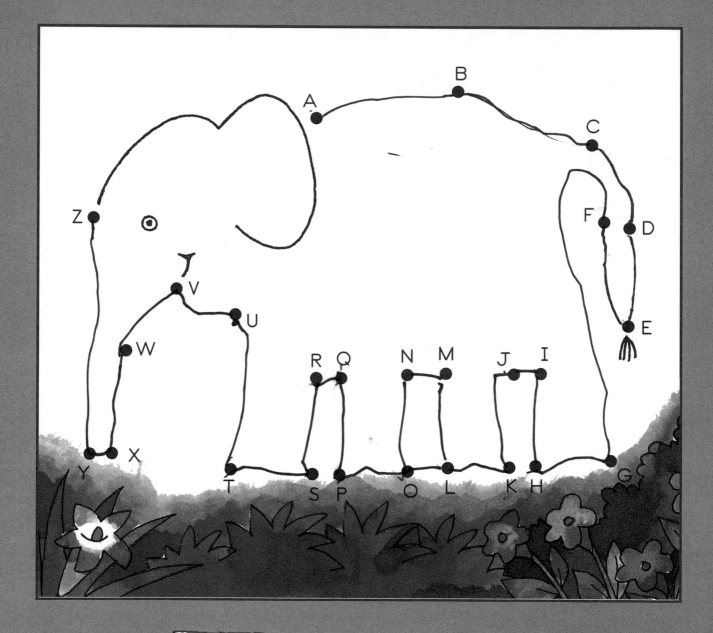

**Skills:** Identifying objects that begin with the **e** sound; distinguishing between long and short **e** sounds

Sometimes the letter **e** makes a different sound. The word **eat** starts with a long **e** sound. Can you say **eat?** Draw a picture of your favorite thing to eat.

# I Is for Igloo and Ice

Say the name of each picture. Circle the picture that starts with the short **i** sound that you hear in the word **in.**

Sometimes the letter **i** makes a different sound. The word **ice** starts with a long **i** sound. Can you say **ice?**

**Ice cream** begins with the long **i** sound. Fill this ice-cream cone by drawing a scoop of your favorite ice-cream flavor on top.

# O Is for Olive and Oval

The word **olive** starts with a short **o** sound. Can you say **olive?**

What else starts with the short **o** sound? Look at the picture. Color all the spaces marked with an **o** to find out.

**Skills:** Identifying objects that begin with the **o** sound; distinguishing between long and short **o** sounds

Sometimes the letter **o** makes a different sound. The word **oval** starts with a long **o** sound. Can you say **oval?** Draw a picture of your favorite toy in this oval.

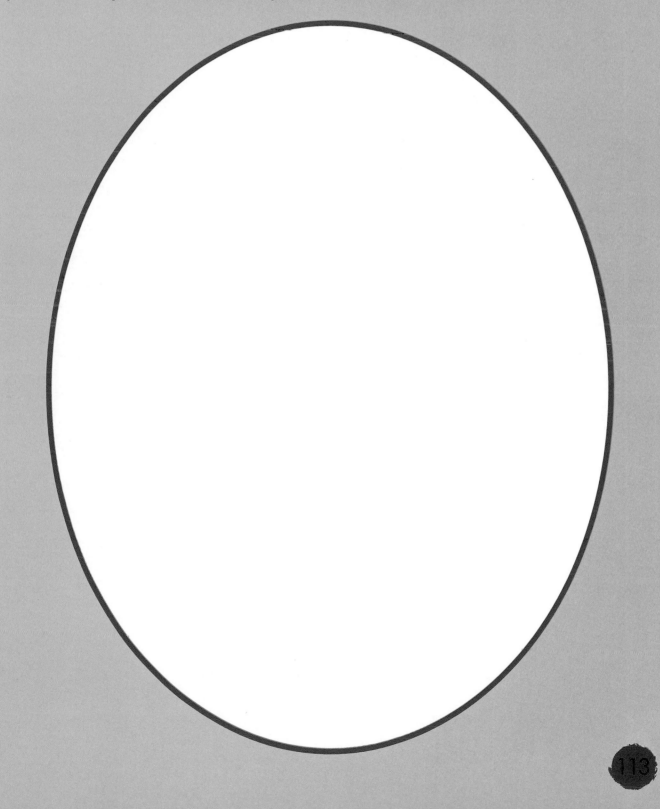

# U Is for Umbrella and Uniform

The word **umbrella** starts with a short **u** sound. Can you say **umbrella?** Look at the picture. Can you find four umbrellas? Put a circle around each umbrella.

Sometimes the letter **u** makes a different sound. The word **uniform** starts with the long **u** sound. Can you say **uniform?** Draw a circle around each person who is wearing a uniform.

# Vowel Review

Say the name of the picture at the beginning of each row.
Then circle the letter you hear at the beginning of the word.

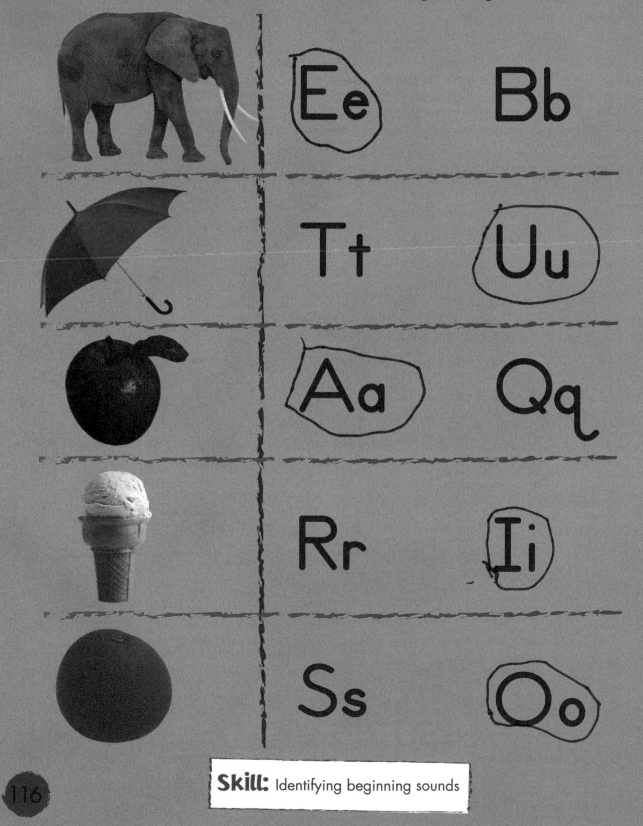

| | | |
|---|---|---|
| 🐘 | (Ee) | Bb |
| ☂ | Tt | (Uu) |
| 🍎 | (Aa) | Qq |
| 🍦 | Rr | (Ii) |
| 🟠 | Ss | (Oo) |

**Skill:** Identifying beginning sounds

# Rhyming Pictures

A **rhyme** is when two words have the same sound at the end. Say the names of the pictures. Circle the picture in each row that rhymes with the first picture.

**Skill:** Identifying rhyming sounds

# More Rhyming Pictures

Say the names of the pictures. Circle the picture in each row that rhymes with the first picture.

# What Happens Next?

Draw a line from each picture on the left to the picture on the right that shows what comes next.

# First, Second, Last!

Some things happen in order. Look at the pictures in each column. Write numbers in the boxes to show what happened first, second, and last. The first one is done for you.

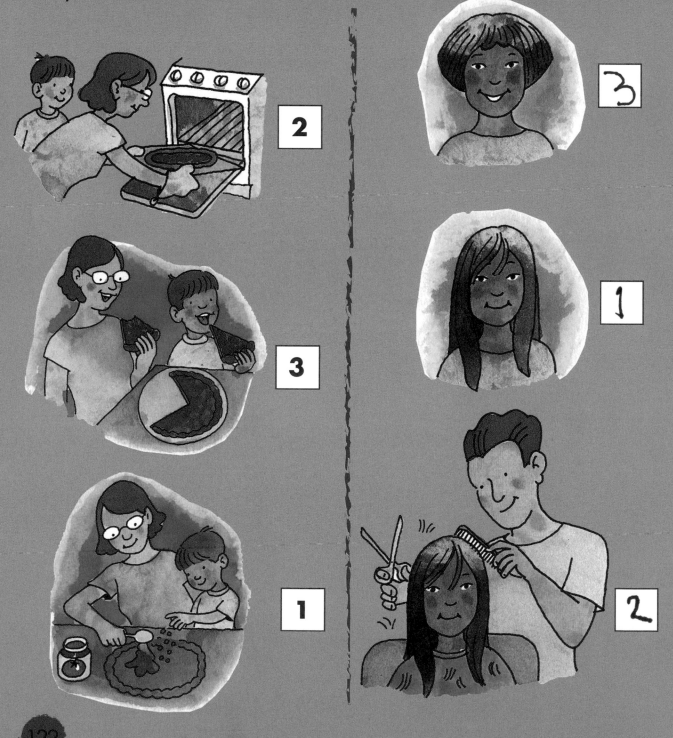

**Skill:** Sequencing

# Your Own Story

Use the boxes to draw your own story! Draw what happened first in the first box and what happened next in the second box.

**Skill:** Sequencing

# What's the Story?

Look at the picture and tell a story about what is happening.
Tell as many things that are happening as you can.

**Skill:** Using a picture to tell a story

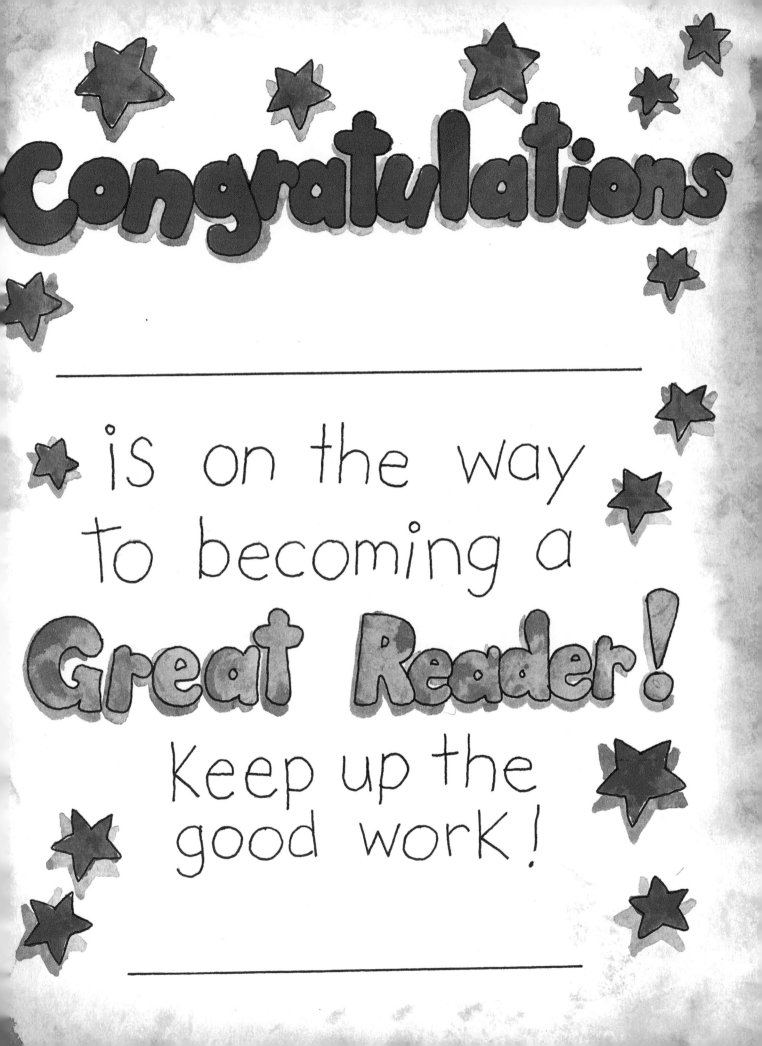

# Congratulations

_____

is on the way
to becoming a

## Great Reader!

Keep up the
good work!

_____